GIRLS GRATITUDE
Journal

THIS BELONGS TO:

Free Audio

7-Minute Gratitude Meditation for Girls
including 8 powerful affirmations!

<u>Link in the back of the book</u>

Scholastic Panda
Education

ISBN: 978-1-953149-41-1

HELLO YOU WONDERFUL HUMAN...

This journal is a safe and private place to share your thoughts and uniqueness.

Each page is filled with fun ways for you to freely express your opinions, creativity, and become more aware of yourself.

Of course, do not forget to color all of the beautiful artwork and make it your own!

DID YOU KNOW THAT COLORING CAN HELP RELAX YOUR MIND AND REDUCE STRESS? NOT TO MENTION IT'S REALLY FUN!

Spending just a few minutes to write and color in your journal each day will help to calm your mind, fill your heart with love and remind you of all of the things you have to be grateful for.

Don't worry if you forget to write in your journal one day, just remember for the next day and most importantly enjoy this new journey!

I AM THANKFUL FOR...

FAMILY

FRIENDS

GOOD WEATHER

MY PET

DELICIOUS FOOD

VACATION

FUN EXPERIENCES

DATE: __/__/__   M   T   W   TH   F   SAT   SUN

I AM A GREAT FRIEND

TODAY I AM THANKFUL FOR... _____

THE LAST TIME I LAUGHED WAS... _____

"BE INSPIRED BY THE SUCCESS OF OTHERS"

I FEEL: 😄 🙂 🙂 😐 🙁 ☹️ 😠

COLOR YOUR MOOD TODAY

DATE: ___ / ___ / ___   M   T   W   TH   F   SAT   SUN

I AM A GOOD REASON FOR TODAY TO EXIST

THE LAST PERSON I SAID "I LOVE YOU" TO WAS... _____

TODAY IS GOING TO BE WONDERFUL BECAUSE... _____

_____

I FEEL: 😄 🙂 🙂 😐 🙁 ☹️ 😠

COLOR YOUR MOOD TODAY

DATE: ___/___/___   M   T   W   TH   F   SAT   SUN

I FEEL: 😄 🙂 🙂 😐 🙁 ☹️ 😦

COLOR YOUR MOOD TODAY

Relax And Color

I'M THANKFUL FOR TODAY BECAUSE... _____

EXPRESS YOUR EMOTIONS WITH COLOR

DATE: ___/___/___   M   T   W   TH   F   SAT   SUN

I AM INDEPENDENT

An important change I'm grateful I've made recently is:

_____

_____

"I AM SURROUNDED BY LOVE"

I Feel: 😄 🙂 🙂 😐 🙁 🙁 ☹️

COLOR YOUR MOOD TODAY

DATE: ___/___/___   M   T   W   TH   F   SAT   SUN

TIME TO LET GO

IN EACH BALLOON WRITE SOMETHING THAT MAKES YOU FEEL UPSET OR ANXIOUS. THEN CLOSE YOUR EYES AND IMAGINE LETTING IT FLY AWAY!!

COLOR EACH BALLOON TOO!

I AM IMPORTANT

I FEEL: 😄 🙂 🙂 😐 🙁 ☹️ 😦

COLOR YOUR MOOD TODAY

DATE: ___ / ___ / ___   M   T   W   TH   F   SAT   SUN

I HAVE A HEART OF GOLD

One thing I like about my neighborhood..._____

_____

Because... _____

_____

"I AM THE BEST DAUGHTER ANYONE COULD HAVE"

I Feel: 😀 🙂 🙂 😐 🙁 ☹️ 😣

COLOR YOUR MOOD TODAY

DATE: ___/___/___   M   T   W   TH   F   SAT   SUN

✦ TODAY, I CHOOSE ME ✦

WHAT I LIKE MOST ABOUT MY BODY IS...

_____

BECAUSE...

_____

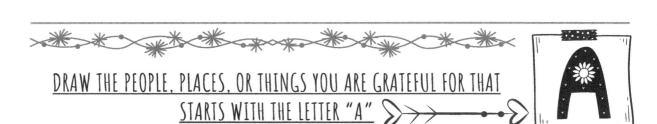

DRAW THE PEOPLE, PLACES, OR THINGS YOU ARE GRATEFUL FOR THAT
STARTS WITH THE LETTER "A" ➤➤➤➤

TODAY I'M THANKFUL FOR _____

_____

I FEEL: 😀 🙂 🙂 😐 🙁 🙁 ☹️

COLOR YOUR MOOD TODAY

DATE: ___/___/___   M   T   W   TH   F   SAT   SUN

MY WORDS MATTER

A MISTAKE I AM GRATEFUL FOR IS... _____

_____

BECAUSE I LEARNED... _____

_____

"MY MISTAKES DON'T DEFINE ME"

I FEEL: 😄 🙂 🙂 😐 🙁 ☹️ 😧

COLOR YOUR MOOD TODAY

I COMPLETELY AND HONESTLY LOVE AND ACCEPT MYSELF

THE LAST TIME I PRACTICED FORGIVENESS WAS..._____

_____

AFTERWARDS I FELT..._____

_____

"I AM FUN TO BE AROUND"

I FEEL: 😄 🙂 🙂 😐 🙁 ☹️ 😞

COLOR YOUR MOOD TODAY

DATE: ___/___/___   M   T   W   TH   F   SAT   SUN

SMILING IS GOOD FOR THE SOUL

ACT OF GRATITUDE

STUDIES HAVE SHOWN THAT SMILING HAS THE POWER TO RELIEVE ANXIETY, STRENGTHEN RELATIONSHIPS, AND EVEN REDUCE YOUR RISK OF HEART DISEASE.

LIST 5 THINGS THAT ALWAYS MAKE YOU SMILE

1 _____
2 _____
3 _____
4 _____
5 _____

BEING SMART IS AN AMAZING FEELING

I FEEL: 😀 🙂 🙂 😐 🙁 ☹️ 😞

COLOR YOUR MOOD TODAY

DATE: ___/___/___   M   T   W   TH   F   SAT   SUN

I AM INTELLIGENT

THE BEST THING ABOUT TODAY
(DRAW OR WRITE)

A PERSON I AM GRATEFUL FOR... _____

BECAUSE... _____

A MEMORY I AM GRATEFUL FOR... _____

I FEEL: 😀   🙂   🙂   😐   🙁   ☹️   😧

COLOR YOUR MOOD TODAY

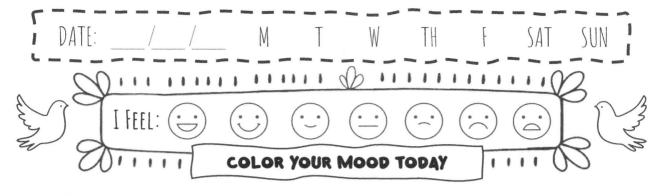

DATE: ___/___/___   M   T   W   TH   F   SAT   SUN

I FEEL: 😄 🙂 🙂 😐 ☹️ 🙁 😦

COLOR YOUR MOOD TODAY

A TALENT I'M THANKFUL FOR... _____

THERE IS JOY IN ME

DATE: ___/___/___   M   T   W   TH   F   SAT   SUN

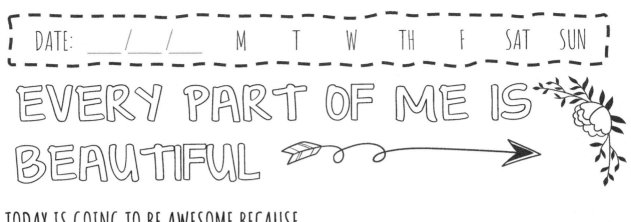

EVERY PART OF ME IS BEAUTIFUL

TODAY IS GOING TO BE AWESOME BECAUSE... _____

_____

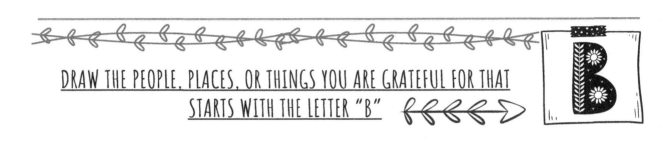

DRAW THE PEOPLE, PLACES, OR THINGS YOU ARE GRATEFUL FOR THAT STARTS WITH THE LETTER "B"

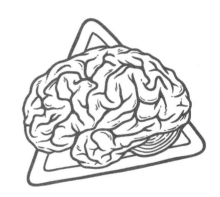

I FEEL: 😄 🙂 🙂 😐 🙁 🙁 ☹️

COLOR YOUR MOOD TODAY

DATE: ___/___/___   M   T   W   TH   F   SAT   SUN

Time To Pay It Forward

WHAT ARE <u>TWO</u> ACTS OF KINDNESS YOU CAN DO TODAY
FOR TWO PEOPLE YOU DON'T KNOW?

I AM IMPORTANT

I FEEL:

COLOR YOUR MOOD TODAY

TEACHERS ARE EVERYWHERE

ACT OF GRATITUDE

TEACHERS AREN'T JUST IN THE CLASSROOM. THINK OF SOMEONE WHO TAUGHT YOU SOMETHING AND <u>TELL THEM HOW GRATEFUL YOU ARE</u>.

THE PERSON I AM GRATEFUL FOR IS... _____

THIS PERSON TAUGHT ME... _____

I KEEP MY BODY HEALTHY

 I FEEL:

COLOR YOUR MOOD TODAY

DATE: ___/___/___ M T W TH F SAT SUN

MY FEELINGS MATTER

TODAY IS GOING TO BE GREAT BECAUSE... _____

_____

MY FAVORITE TYPE OF MUSIC IS... _____

BECAUSE... _____

"I CHOOSE TO FEEL HAPPY"

I FEEL: 😄 🙂 🙂 😐 🙁 ☹️ 😫

COLOR YOUR MOOD TODAY

DATE: ___/___/___   M   T   W   TH   F   SAT   SUN

EVERYTHING WILL BE OKAY

SOMETHING HELPFUL I WISH I COULD DO MORE OFTEN IS... _____

_____

DRAW THE PEOPLE, PLACES, OR THINGS YOU ARE GRATEFUL FOR THAT STARTS WITH THE LETTER "C"

C

I FEEL: 😃 🙂 🙂 😐 🙁 ☹️ 😣

COLOR YOUR MOOD TODAY

DATE: ___/___/___   M   T   W   TH   F   SAT   SUN

I AM OPEN TO LEARNING NEW THINGS

THIS WEEK I AM GOING TO IMPROVE ON..._____

I FEEL: 😃 🙂 🙂 😐 😕 🙁 ☹️

COLOR YOUR MOOD TODAY

DATE: ___/___/___   M   T   W   TH   F   SAT   SUN

I AM HONEST

WHAT IS YOUR FAVORITE PET? (DRAW OR WRITE)

TODAY I AM GRATEFUL FOR... _____

_____

BECAUSE... _____

_____

I FEEL:

COLOR YOUR MOOD TODAY

DATE: ___/___/___ M T W TH F SAT SUN

I AM BEAUTIFUL

WHAT IS YOUR FAVORITE THING TO DO OUTSIDE? DRAW BELOW.

COLOR IT TOO!

THIS YEAR I WANT TO GET BETTER AT... _____

_____

THIS IS IMPORTANT TO ME BECAUSE... _____

_____

"IT'S OK TO ASK FOR HELP"

I FEEL: 😄 🙂 🙂 😐 🙁 🙁 😟

COLOR YOUR MOOD TODAY

DATE: ___/___/___   M   T   W   TH   F   SAT   SUN

TODAY I WILL LEARN AND GROW

TODAY IS GOING TO BE AWESOME BECAUSE... _____

_____

DRAW THE PEOPLE, PLACES, OR THINGS YOU ARE GRATEFUL FOR THAT
STARTS WITH THE LETTER "U"

I FEEL:

COLOR YOUR MOOD TODAY

THERE IS NOTHING I CAN'T DO

TODAY I AM THANKFUL FOR... _____

DRAW YOURSELF AND A FRIEND YOU ARE MOST GRATEFUL FOR.

I FEEL:

COLOR YOUR MOOD TODAY

DATE: ___/___/___   M   T   W   TH   F   SAT   SUN

I AM NOT A FAILURE

MY FAVORITE TIME OF THE DAY IS... _____

BECAUSE... _____

DESCRIBE YOURSELF IN THREE WORDS... _____

DRAW THE PEOPLE, PLACES, OR THINGS YOU ARE GRATEFUL FOR THAT STARTS WITH THE LETTER "Y"

I FEEL:

COLOR YOUR MOOD TODAY

DATE: ___/___/___   M   T   W   TH   F   SAT   SUN

USE YOUR SUPERPOWERS

ACT OF GRATITUDE

WHICH OF YOUR SKILLS ARE YOU GRATEFUL FOR?

FOR EACH SKILL THINK OF AN IDEA ON HOW YOU CAN USE IT TO HELP SOMEONE ELSE!

MY SKILLS

IDEAS TO HELP OTHERS

1.

2.

3.

I CAN ADAPT TO ANYTHING

I FEEL: 😀 🙂 🙂 😐 🙁 ☹️ 😞

COLOR YOUR MOOD TODAY

DATE: ___/___/___   M   T   W   TH   F   SAT   SUN

I LOVE AND APPROVE OF MYSELF

THE LAST GIFT I RECEIVED WAS... _____

_____

TODAY IS GOING TO BE GREAT BECAUSE... _____

_____

"THERE IS JOY IN YOU"

I FEEL: 😄 🙂 🙂 😐 🙁 ☹️ 😦

COLOR YOUR MOOD TODAY

DATE: ___/___/___   M   T   W   TH   F   SAT   SUN

"THE MOST CERTAIN WAY TO SUCCEED IS TO TRY ONE MORE TIME"

WHEN I NEED TO TAKE A BREAK FROM DOING SOMETHING DIFFICULT I LIKE TO DO...

_____

_____

I FEEL:

COLOR YOUR MOOD TODAY

I EMBRACE MY POWER

A GOOD DEED I DID TODAY WAS... _____

_____

DRAW THE PEOPLE, PLACES, OR THINGS YOU ARE GRATEFUL FOR THAT
STARTS WITH THE LETTER "E"

E

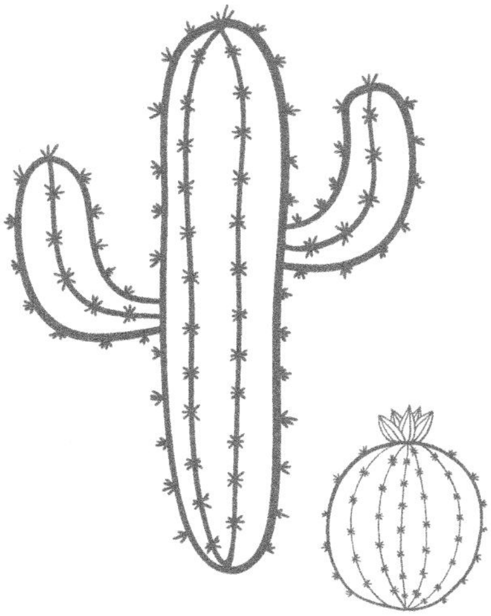

I FEEL: 😃 🙂 🙂 😐 🙁 ☹️ 😣

COLOR YOUR MOOD TODAY

DATE: ___/___/___   M   T   W   TH   F   SAT   SUN

I CAN REACH MY DREAMS

IF I COULD GO BACK IN TIME I WOULD GO TO... _____

_____

I AM GOING TO MAKE TODAY GREAT BY... _____

_____

"I LIKE TO KEEP TRYING, EVEN WHEN THINGS ARE HARD"

I FEEL:

COLOR YOUR MOOD TODAY

DATE: ___/___/___ M T W TH F SAT SUN

WORDS ARE POWERFUL

ACT OF GRATITUDE

WRITE A THANK YOU NOTE TO SOMEONE SPECIAL AND SURPRISE THEM!

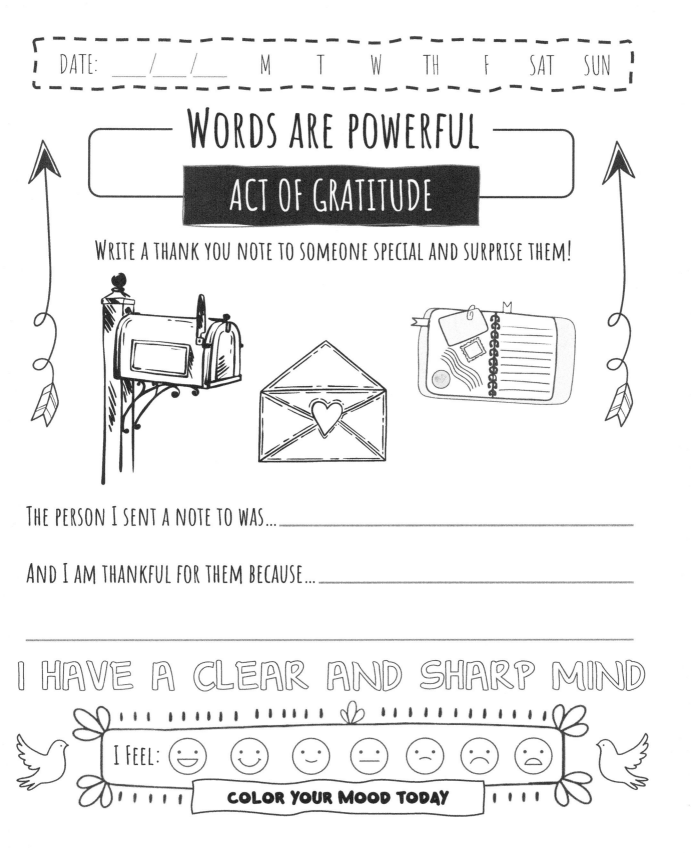

THE PERSON I SENT A NOTE TO WAS... _____

AND I AM THANKFUL FOR THEM BECAUSE... _____

_____

I HAVE A CLEAR AND SHARP MIND

I FEEL: 😄 🙂 🙂 😐 🙁 🙁 😦

COLOR YOUR MOOD TODAY

I CAN ACHIEVE ANYTHING

I AM THANKFUL I CAN... _____

_____

THE LAST TIME I WAS SURPRISED... _____

_____

"I AM WORTHY OF AMAZING THINGS"

I FEEL: 😀 🙂 🙂 😐 😕 🙁 😧

COLOR YOUR MOOD TODAY

I GIVE MYSELF ROOM
TO GROW

A FEAR I PLAN TO OVERCOME THIS YEAR IS... _____

_____

DRAW THE PEOPLE, PLACES, OR THINGS YOU ARE GRATEFUL FOR THAT
STARTS WITH THE LETTER "F"

F

I FEEL: 😄 🙂 🙂 😐 🙁 ☹️ 😟

COLOR YOUR MOOD TODAY

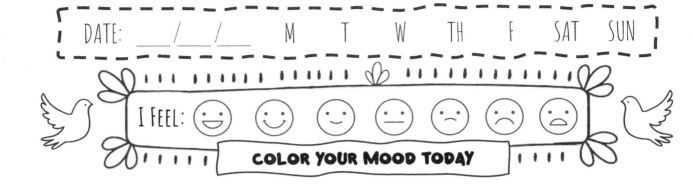

DATE: ___ / ___ / ___   M   T   W   TH   F   SAT   SUN

I FEEL: 😀 🙂 🙂 😐 🙁 ☹️ 😫

COLOR YOUR MOOD TODAY

I'M THANKFUL FOR TODAY BECAUSE... _____

"I AM ALLOWED TO FEEL PROUD OF MYSELF"

DATE: ___ / ___ / ___   M   T   W   TH   F   SAT   SUN

I AM LOVED

WHAT ARE YOU PASSIONATE ABOUT? (DRAW OR WRITE)

TODAY I AM GRATEFUL FOR...

BECAUSE...

I FEEL: 😄 🙂 🙂 😐 🙁 ☹️ 😠

COLOR YOUR MOOD TODAY

Create A Vision Board

ACT OF GRATITUDE

LOOK THROUGH MAGAZINES OR TAKE YOUR OWN PICTURES TO CREATE A COLLAGE OR VISION BOARD OF THINGS THAT MAKE YOU FEEL THANKFUL!

PROGRESS

HAPPINESS

INSPIRATION

DREAMS

FAMILY

TRAVEL

GLUE

I WANT TO TRY

MY FUTURE IS BRIGHT

I FEEL:

COLOR YOUR MOOD TODAY

I AM WORTHY OF A WONDERFUL LIFE

THE LAST PROBLEM I SOLVED WAS... _____

_____

AND I WAS THANKFUL BECAUSE... _____

_____

"I ALWAYS SEE THE GOOD IN PEOPLE, INCLUDING MYSELF"

I FEEL: 😄 🙂 🙂 😐 🙁 🙁 ☹️

COLOR YOUR MOOD TODAY

DATE: ___/___/___ M T W TH F SAT SUN

I AM A WINNER

DRAW OR WRITE YOUR FAVORITE BOOK.
WHAT DO YOU LIKE ABOUT IT?

A TIME I ASKED FOR HELP... _____

_____

AND I WAS GRATEFUL BECAUSE... _____

_____

I FEEL: 😃 🙂 🙂 😐 🙁 🙁 ☹️

COLOR YOUR MOOD TODAY

DATE: ___/___/___   M   T   W   TH   F   SAT   SUN

"I AM NOT RESPONSIBLE FOR HOW OTHER PEOPLE TALK OR ACT"

I'M THANKFUL FOR TODAY BECAUSE... _____

I FEEL: 😀 🙂 🙂 😐 🙁 🙁 🙁

COLOR YOUR MOOD TODAY

DATE: ___/___/___ M T W TH F SAT SUN

IT'S OKAY FOR ME TO HAVE FUN

WHAT I LOVE ABOUT MY FAMILY THE MOST... _____

DRAW THE PEOPLE, PLACES, OR THINGS YOU ARE GRATEFUL FOR THAT STARTS WITH THE LETTER "J"

I FEEL:

COLOR YOUR MOOD TODAY

DATE: ___ / ___ / ___   M   T   W   TH   F   SAT   SUN

A Wall of Gratitude

ACT OF GRATITUDE

Each night think of one simple thing you are thankful for.
Write it on an index card or sticky note and hang on the wall.

I LIKE TO HELP MY FAMILY

I FEEL: 😀 🙂 🙂 😐 🙁 🙁 🙁

COLOR YOUR MOOD TODAY

DATE: ___/___/___   M   T   W   TH   F   SAT   SUN

I LEARN FROM MY MISTAKES

ONE THING I LOVE ABOUT MY FAMILY... _____

I ALWAYS SMILE WHEN I SEE... _____

"I BELIEVE IN MY TALENTS AND SKILLS"

I FEEL:

COLOR YOUR MOOD TODAY

I AM BALANCED

MY FAVORITE FAMILY TRADITION IS... _____

_____

WHAT I LOVE ABOUT IT IS... _____

_____

DRAW THE PEOPLE, PLACES, OR THINGS YOU ARE GRATEFUL FOR THAT
STARTS WITH THE LETTER "W"

W

I FEEL: 😄 🙂 🙂 😐 🙁 🙁 😦

COLOR YOUR MOOD TODAY

I DON'T LET THINGS BOTHER ME

ONE OF MY EARLIEST MEMORIES IS... _____

_____

TODAY IS SPECIAL BECAUSE... _____

_____

"I TREAT OTHERS AS I WANT TO BE TREATED"

I FEEL:

COLOR YOUR MOOD TODAY

DATE: ___/___/___   M   T   W   TH   F   SAT   SUN

MY LIFE IS A GIFT

THE LAST TIME I GAVE SOMEONE A COMPLIMENT WAS... _____

_____

DRAW THE PEOPLE, PLACES, OR THINGS YOU ARE GRATEFUL FOR THAT STARTS WITH THE LETTER "G"

RADIATE POSITIVITY

I FEEL:

COLOR YOUR MOOD TODAY

NATURE IS BEAUTIFUL

ACT OF GRATITUDE

TAKE A NATURE WALK TO APPRECIATE ALL THE AMAZING THINGS AROUND US WE OFTEN TAKE FOR GRANTED. SHARE YOUR EXPERIENCE BELOW!

PEOPLE SEE ME AS CONFIDENT

I FEEL: 😀 🙂 🙂 😐 🙁 🙁 🙁

COLOR YOUR MOOD TODAY

DATE: ___/___/___   M   T   W   TH   F   SAT   SUN

I AM CAPABLE

A MISTAKE I AM GRATEFUL FOR IS... _____

_____

BECAUSE I LEARNED... _____

_____

"I KNOW THAT BABY STEPS ADD UP TO BIG STEPS"

I FEEL: :D :) :) :| :(:(:(

COLOR YOUR MOOD TODAY

WITH EVERY BREATH OUT, I RELEASE STRESS IN MY BODY

THE BEST THING ABOUT MY WEEK SO FAR IS... _____

_____

DRAW THE PEOPLE, PLACES, OR THINGS YOU ARE GRATEFUL FOR THAT STARTS WITH THE LETTER "Z"

Z

I FEEL: 😀 🙂 🙂 😐 🙁 ☹️ 😣

COLOR YOUR MOOD TODAY

DATE: ___/___/___   M   T   W   TH   F   SAT   SUN

I HAVE EVERYTHING I NEED

TODAY IS SPECIAL BECAUSE... _____

_____

MY FAVORITE MEAL OF THE DAY IS:

Breakfast   Lunch   Dinner

BECAUSE... _____

"I DESERVE RESPECT"

I FEEL: 😄 🙂 🙂 😐 🙁 ☹️ 😣

COLOR YOUR MOOD TODAY

DATE: ___/___/___ M T W TH F SAT SUN

THE UNIVERSE IS LOOKING OUT FOR ME

ONE THING I LIKE ABOUT MY SCHOOL IS... _____

DRAW THE PEOPLE, PLACES, OR THINGS YOU ARE GRATEFUL FOR THAT
STARTS WITH THE LETTER "X"

I FEEL:

COLOR YOUR MOOD TODAY

DATE: ___/___/___   M   T   W   TH   F   SAT   SUN

THE MONTH IN REVIEW

ACT OF GRATITUDE

TWO IMPORTANT THINGS THAT HAPPENED THIS MONTH I AM GRATEFUL FOR...

1

_____

_____

_____

2

_____

_____

_____

DRAW THE THING I AM MOST GRATEFUL FOR THIS MONTH

I CAN ADAPT TO ANYTHING

I FEEL: 😀 🙂 🙂 😐 🙁 ☹️ ☹️

COLOR YOUR MOOD TODAY

I'M THANKFUL FOR TODAY BECAUSE... _____

"PEOPLE SEE ME AS A CONFIDENT"

I FEEL:

COLOR YOUR MOOD TODAY

DATE: ___ / ___ / ___   M   T   W   TH   F   SAT   SUN

I'M HAPPY WITH WHO I AM

TODAY IS SPECIAL BECAUSE... _____

_____

"THE THINGS THAT MAKE ME DIFFERENT ARE THE THINGS THAT MAKE ME ME"

I FEEL:

COLOR YOUR MOOD TODAY

DATE: ___/___/___   M   T   W   TH   F   SAT   SUN

MY GOALS ARE ACHIEVABLE

SOMETHING I AM WORRIED ABOUT LATELY IS... _____

_____

I WILL OVERCOME THIS BY... _____

DRAW THE PEOPLE, PLACES, OR THINGS YOU ARE GRATEFUL FOR THAT
STARTS WITH THE LETTER "T"

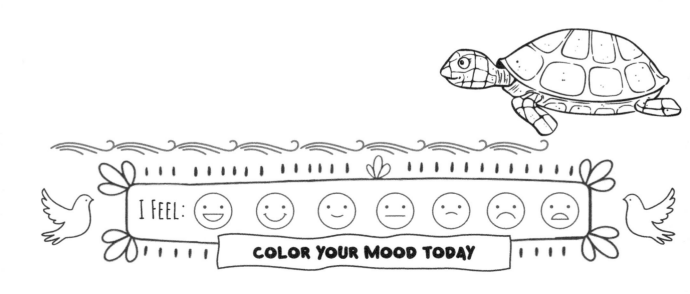

I FEEL:

COLOR YOUR MOOD TODAY

DATE: ___/___/___   M   T   W   TH   F   SAT   SUN

I CREATE JOY FOR OTHERS EVERY DAY

I AM EXCITED FOR TODAY BECAUSE... _____

My FAVORITE SEASON OF THE YEAR IS:

Winter   Fall   Spring   Summer

BECAUSE... _____

I FEEL: 😄 🙂 🙂 😐 🙁 ☹️ ☹️

COLOR YOUR MOOD TODAY

DATE: ___/___/___   M   T   W   TH   F   SAT   SUN

MY LIFE IS FILLED WITH POSITIVE THINGS

THREE THINGS MY FRIENDS AND I ENJOY DOING TOGETHER...

① _____

② _____

③ _____

I FEEL: 😀 🙂 🙂 😐 😕 🙁 ☹️

COLOR YOUR MOOD TODAY

DATE: ___/___/___   M   T   W   TH   F   SAT   SUN

So Much To Be Grateful for

ACT OF GRATITUDE

Being alive is a beautiful gift!
Color each word that you are thankful for

ELECTRICITY
INVENTORS
EYESIGHT
DIVERSITY
RAINBOWS
CLEAN WATER
CAMPFIRES
ART
FAMILY
MUSIC
SUNSETS
TECHNOLOGY
PETS
SUNSHINE
LAUGHTER
CHALLENGES
EDUCATION
HOLIDAYS
NATURE
FRIENDS

I FEEL:

COLOR YOUR MOOD TODAY

DATE: ___/___/___   M   T   W   TH   F   SAT   SUN

I SPEAK TO MYSELF
WITH KINDNESS

THE LAST FUNNY JOKE I HEARD WAS... _____

_____

_____

A MOMENT I REALLY ENJOYED TODAY... _____

_____

I FEEL: 😄 🙂 🙂 😐 🙁 🙁 ☹️

COLOR YOUR MOOD TODAY

DATE: ___/___/___   M   T   W   TH   F   SAT   SUN

I FEARLESSLY APPROACH OTHERS

MY FAVORITE ACTIVITY TO DO INSIDE IS... _____

_____

A MOMENT I REALLY ENJOYED TODAY... _____

_____

I FEEL: 😄 🙂 🙂 😐 🙁 ☹️ ☹️

COLOR YOUR MOOD TODAY

DATE: ___/___/___   M   T   W   TH   F   SAT   SUN

I WILL TURN NEGATIVE
THOUGHTS INTO POSITIVE ONES

I SHOW OTHER PEOPLE I CARE ABOUT THEM BY... _____

_____

DRAW THE PEOPLE, PLACES, OR THINGS YOU ARE GRATEFUL FOR THAT
STARTS WITH THE LETTER "K"

I FEEL: 😄   🙂   🙂   😐   🙁   ☹️   😠

COLOR YOUR MOOD TODAY

DATE: ___/___/___   M   T   W   TH   F   SAT   SUN

SOMETHING I DIDN'T THINK I WOULD LIKE, BUT ACTUALLY ENJOYED WAS... _____

_____

I CAN ALWAYS BE MYSELF, NO MATTER THE SITUATION

I FEEL: 😀 🙂 🙂 😐 🙁 ☹️ 😦

COLOR YOUR MOOD TODAY

GRATITUDE MEDITATION

ACT OF GRATITUDE

1. FIND A QUIET PLACE TO SIT COMFORTABLY ON THE FLOOR OR A CHAIR FOR FIVE MINUTES AND CLOSE YOUR EYES.
2. TAKE THREE DEEP BREATHS IN AND SLOWLY EXHALE OUT YOUR NOSE.
3. RELAX YOUR MIND AND THINK ABOUT ALL THE PEOPLE AND THINGS YOU ARE GRATEFUL FOR.

I AM NEVER ALONE

I FEEL: 😀 🙂 🙂 😐 🙁 🙁 ☹️

COLOR YOUR MOOD TODAY

DATE: ___/___/___   M   T   W   TH   F   SAT   SUN

I AM FOCUSING ON THE POSITIVE TODAY

MY DREAM VACATION WOULD BE... _____

_____

DRAW THE PEOPLE, PLACES, OR THINGS YOU ARE GRATEFUL FOR THAT STARTS WITH THE LETTER "O"

I FEEL: 😄 🙂 🙂 😐 🙁 ☹️ 😦

COLOR YOUR MOOD TODAY

DATE: ___/___/___   M   T   W   TH   F   SAT   SUN

MY CHARM IS
UNIVERSAL

Draw something that makes you happy

Some people who are really good listeners in my life are... _____

_____

"I COMMUNICATE WITH HONESTY"

I FEEL: 😀 🙂 ☺ 😐 🙁 ☹ 😠

COLOR YOUR MOOD TODAY

DATE: ___/___/___   M   T   W   TH   F   SAT   SUN

I AM KIND TO ALL THOSE AROUND ME

WHO LOVES AND CARES FOR YOU? _____

TODAY I'M THANKFUL FOR... _____

I FEEL: 😃 🙂 🙂 😐 🙁 ☹️ 😣

COLOR YOUR MOOD TODAY

DATE: ___/___/___ M   T   W   TH   F   SAT   SUN

I GIVE UP THE HABIT OF CRITICIZING MYSELF

A PLACE I FEEL REALLY SAFE IS... _____

_____

DRAW THE PEOPLE, PLACES, OR THINGS YOU ARE GRATEFUL FOR THAT STARTS WITH THE LETTER "Q"

I FEEL: 😃 🙂 🙂 😐 🙁 🙁 ☹️

COLOR YOUR MOOD TODAY

DATE: ___/___/___   M   T   W   TH   F   SAT   SUN

MAKE A GRATITUDE JAR

ACT OF GRATITUDE

Fill your gratitude jar with notes of all the things you're grateful for. Come back and review your jar full of reasons to be grateful whenever you need some inspiration or feeling blue.

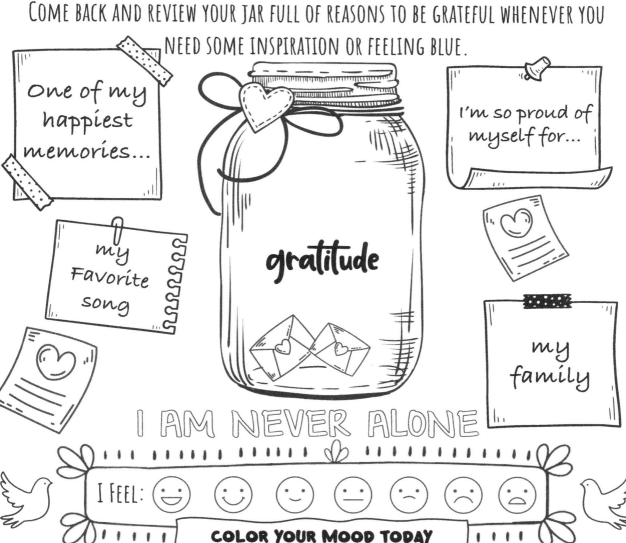

One of my happiest memories...

I'm so proud of myself for...

my Favorite song

gratitude

my family

I AM NEVER ALONE

I Feel: 😀 🙂 🙂 😐 🙁 ☹️ ☹️

COLOR YOUR MOOD TODAY

I AM COMFORTABLE IN MY OWN SKIN

WHEN I'M SAD I CAN ALWAYS COUNT ON... _____

TWO THINGS I AM THANKFUL FOR TODAY

① _____

② _____

I FEEL: 😀 🙂 🙂 😐 🙁 🙁 ☹️

COLOR YOUR MOOD TODAY

I MAKE TIME FOR MY FRIENDS

SOMETHING I DID EVEN THOUGH IT WAS SCARY WAS... _____

DRAW THE PEOPLE, PLACES, OR THINGS YOU ARE GRATEFUL FOR THAT STARTS WITH THE LETTER "S"

I FEEL: 😄   🙂   🙂   😐   🙁   🙁   🙁

COLOR YOUR MOOD TODAY

DATE: ___ / ___ / ___   M   T   W   TH   F   SAT   SUN

I ATTRACT GOOD FORTUNE

IF YOU COULD SPEAK ANY LANGUAGE FLUENTLY, WHAT WOULD IT BE?

_____

THIS PERSON WAS KIND TO ME TODAY:

_____

TWO THINGS I AM THANKFUL FOR TODAY

① _____

② _____

I FEEL: 😄 🙂 🙂 😐 🙁 ☹️ 😞

COLOR YOUR MOOD TODAY

DATE: ___/___/___ M T W TH F SAT SUN

I PRACTICE PATIENCE

EVERYDAY IS AN OPPORTUNITY TO EXPRESS GRATITUDE.
WRITE SOMETHING GOOD THAT HAPPENED FOR EACH DAY OF THE WEEK

MONDAY

TUESDAY

FRIDAY

THURSDAY

WEDNESDAY

SUNDAY

SATURDAY

I FEEL: 😃 🙂 🙂 😐 🙁 ☹️ ☹️

COLOR YOUR MOOD TODAY

DATE: ___/___/___   M   T   W   TH   F   SAT   SUN

COMPLIMENTS GO A LONG WAY

ACT OF GRATITUDE

GIVE A FRIEND A GENUINE COMPLIMENT AND MAKE THEIR DAY!

THE PERSON I COMPLIMENTED WAS... _____

AND I AM THANKFUL FOR THEM BECAUSE... _____

_____

I AM CALM AND CONTENT

I FEEL:

COLOR YOUR MOOD TODAY

DATE: ___/___/___   M   T   W   TH   F   SAT   SUN

I DO NOT NEED TO BE FIXED

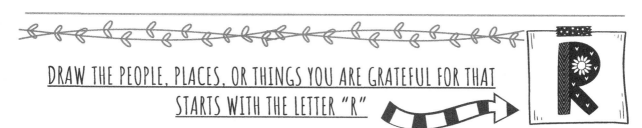

SOMETHING INTERESTING I LEARNED RECENTLY WAS... _____

_____

DRAW THE PEOPLE, PLACES, OR THINGS YOU ARE GRATEFUL FOR THAT STARTS WITH THE LETTER "R"

I FEEL: 😀 🙂 🙂 😐 🙁 🙁 ☹️

COLOR YOUR MOOD TODAY

DATE: ___/___/___   M   T   W   TH   F   SAT   SUN

EVERDAY IS A FRESH START

TODAY I FELT LOVED WHEN... _____

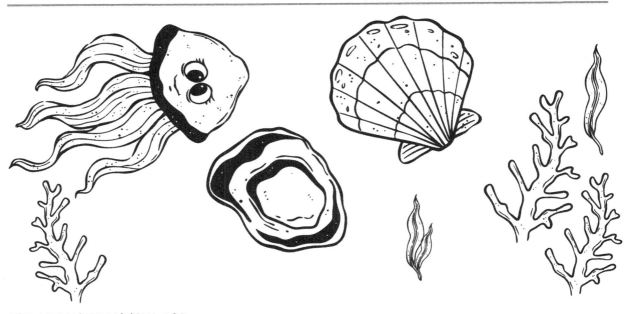

TODAY I'M THANKFUL FOR... _____

I FEEL: 😀 🙂 🙂 😐 🙁 🙁 ☹️

COLOR YOUR MOOD TODAY

DATE: ___/___/___   M   T   W   TH   F   SAT   SUN

I AM THANKFUL FOR
THE LOVE IN MY LIFE

I FEEL HAPPIEST WHEN..._____

_____

DRAW THE PEOPLE, PLACES, OR THINGS YOU ARE GRATEFUL FOR THAT
STARTS WITH THE LETTER "M"

I FEEL: 😄 🙂 🙂 😐 🙁 ☹️ ☹️

COLOR YOUR MOOD TODAY

DATE: ___/___/___   M   T   W   TH   F   SAT   SUN

I LOVE MY BODY AND ALL IT DOES FOR ME

A CHALLENGING PERSON I'M DEALING WITH RIGHT NOW IS

_____

HOWEVER, SOMETHING POSITIVE I'M LEARNING FROM THIS IS

_____

TODAY I'M THANKFUL FOR... _____

_____

I FEEL:

COLOR YOUR MOOD TODAY

GRATITUDE WORD SEARCH

ACT OF GRATITUDE

HOW MANY WORDS CAN YOU FIND BELOW THAT RELATE TO GRATITUDE?

S	N	B	H	Y	W	R	N	Y	Z	G	T
T	T	V	G	O	E	B	L	I	N	E	H
S	O	S	R	S	N	I	I	I	D	K	O
G	T	T	P	P	M	E	V	V	B	W	U
R	H	E	T	A	H	O	S	X	L	G	G
A	C	R	F	S	L	V	R	T	O	N	H
T	S	Q	C	G	I	F	T	P	Y	I	T
E	D	U	T	I	T	A	R	G	A	R	F
F	K	F	R	I	E	N	D	S	L	A	U
U	H	T	L	A	E	H	N	E	T	H	L
L	S	E	D	I	R	P	I	J	Y	S	G
A	X	H	U	L	U	F	K	N	A	H	T

FAMILY
GRATEFUL
HONESTY
LOYALTY
SHARING
WORTH
FRIENDS
GRATITUDE
KIND
PRIDE
THANKFUL
GIFT
HEALTH
LOVING
RESPECT
THOUGHTFUL

MY FAMILY LOVES ME SO MUCH!

I FEEL:

COLOR YOUR MOOD TODAY

I DON'T COMPARE MYSELF TO OTHERS

ONE THING I LOVE ABOUT MY PERSONALITY IS... _____

_____

BECAUSE ... _____

_____

"I RADIATE CONFIDENCE"

I FEEL: 😄 🙂 🙂 😐 🙁 🙁 😞

COLOR YOUR MOOD TODAY

DATE: ___/___/___   M   T   W   TH   F   SAT   SUN

I WILL TRY NEW THINGS

SOMETHING I DID EVEN THOUGH IT WAS DIFFICULT WAS... _____

_____

IT MADE ME FEEL... _____

DRAW THE PEOPLE, PLACES, OR THINGS YOU ARE GRATEFUL FOR THAT
STARTS WITH THE LETTER "L"

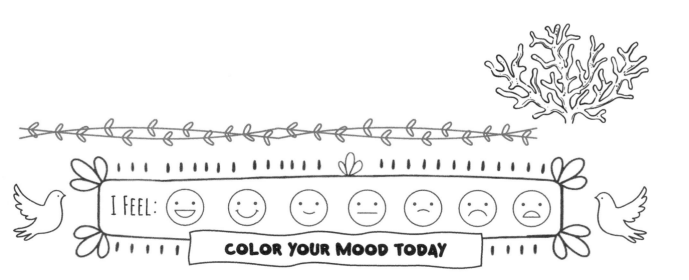

I FEEL: 😃 🙂 😊 😐 🙁 ☹️ 😣

COLOR YOUR MOOD TODAY

I STAND UP FOR WHAT I BELIEVE IN

A DIFFICULT PROBLEM I AM FACING:

I LEARNED:

I LEARNED:

I LEARNED:

TODAY I'M THANKFUL FOR... _____

I FEEL: 😄   🙂   ☺   😐   🙁   ☹   😣

COLOR YOUR MOOD TODAY

DATE: ___/___/___   M   T   W   TH   F   SAT   SUN

"EVERYDAY IS MY BEST DAY"

I'M THANKFUL FOR TODAY BECAUSE... _____

I FEEL: 😀 🙂 🙂 😐 🙁 🙁 ☹️

COLOR YOUR MOOD TODAY

DATE: ___/___/___   M   T   W   TH   F   SAT   SUN

GRATITUDE SCAVENGER HUNT

ACT OF GRATITUDE

Go on a hunt to find things that complete the sentences below

SOMETHING I AM GRATEFUL FOR THAT...

REMINDS ME I AM LOVED

IS USEFUL TO ME

MAKES ME FEEL STRONG

IS MY FAVORITE COLOR

MAKES ME LAUGH

I ENJOY EATING

REMINDS ME OF A BEAUTIFUL MEMORY

I CARE ABOUT OTHERS

I FEEL: 😃 🙂 🙂 😐 🙁 🙁 ☹️

COLOR YOUR MOOD TODAY

hello

DATE: ___/___/___   M   T   W   TH   F   SAT   SUN

I AM THANKFUL

for:

because I can:

because I am:

because I have:

I KNOW MY SELF-WORTH

I Feel: 😀 🙂 🙂 😐 🙁 ☹️ 😟

COLOR YOUR MOOD TODAY

DATE: ___/___/___   M   T   W   TH   F   SAT   SUN

I AM RELAXED AND AT PEACE

SOMETHING THAT MADE ME SMILE TODAY WAS... _____

_____

DRAW THE PEOPLE, PLACES, OR THINGS YOU ARE GRATEFUL FOR THAT
STARTS WITH THE LETTER "H"

I FEEL: 😄 🙂 ☺ 😐 🙁 ☹ 😦

COLOR YOUR MOOD TODAY

TODAY IS MY DAY

CHOOSE A POSITIVE WORD LIKE "HAPPY", "CALM", "FUN", "SURPRISING", OR "BEAUTIFUL" AND WRITE ABOUT A WAY THAT WORD SHOWED UP IN YOUR DAY TODAY.

_____

_____

_____

TWO THINGS I AM THANKFUL FOR TODAY

① _____

② _____

I FEEL: 😀 🙂 🙂 😐 🙁 🙁 ☹️

COLOR YOUR MOOD TODAY

DATE: ___ / ___ / ___   M   T   W   TH   F   SAT   SUN

IT IS ALRIGHT TO FEEL SAD SOMETIMES

TODAY I AM PROUD THAT... _____

_____

FILL IN THE BOXES WITH PLACES YOU WOULD LOVE TO TRAVEL TO

I FEEL: 😄 🙂 ☺ 😐 😕 🙁 ☹

COLOR YOUR MOOD TODAY

DATE: ___/___/___   M   T   W   TH   F   SAT   SUN

Gratitude Plant

ACT OF GRATITUDE

WRITE SOMETHING YOU ARE GRATEFUL FOR IN EACH OF THE PLANT LEAVES BELOW

I AM RESOURCEFUL

I FEEL: ☺ ☺ ☺ ☺ ☹ ☹ ☹

COLOR YOUR MOOD TODAY

DATE: ___/___/___   M   T   W   TH   F   SAT   SUN

I AM ON THE RIGHT PATH FOR ME

THE THINGS MY FRIENDS LIKE THE MOST ABOUT ME ARE... _____

_____

DRAW THE PEOPLE, PLACES, OR THINGS YOU ARE GRATEFUL FOR THAT STARTS WITH THE LETTER "N"

I FEEL: 😀 🙂 🙂 😐 🙁 ☹️ 😧

COLOR YOUR MOOD TODAY

I AM AWARE OF MY STRONG QUALITIES

SOMETHING I WILL IMPROVE ON TODAY... _____

_____

<u>DRAW SOMETHING THAT MAKES YOU HAPPY</u>

TWO THINGS I AM THANKFUL FOR TODAY

① _____

② _____

 I FEEL:

COLOR YOUR MOOD TODAY

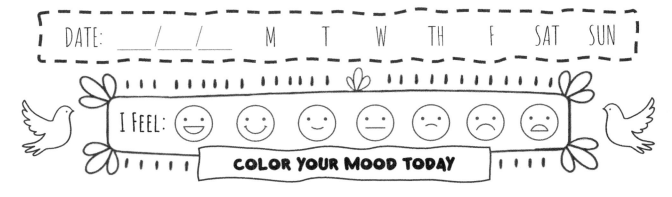

DATE: ___/___/___   M   T   W   TH   F   SAT   SUN

I FEEL: 😄 🙂 🙂 😐 🙁 ☹️ 😣

COLOR YOUR MOOD TODAY

I'M THANKFUL FOR TODAY BECAUSE... _____

"I LISTEN TO OTHERS WITH KINDNESS AND AN OPEN MIND"

I CAN DO ALL THINGS

THE MOST DANGEROUS THING I'VE DONE IS... _____

_____

BUT I LEARNED... _____

DRAW THE PEOPLE, PLACES, OR THINGS YOU ARE GRATEFUL FOR THAT STARTS WITH THE LETTER "V"

I FEEL:

COLOR YOUR MOOD TODAY

DATE: ___/___/___ M T W TH F SAT SUN

A Friendship Bracelet

ACT OF GRATITUDE

Handmade gifts made with love are a great way to show your appreciation to someone you care about.

BUY SOME BEADS AND STRING AND MAKE A FRIENDSHIP BRACELET OR NECKLACE FOR A FRIEND!

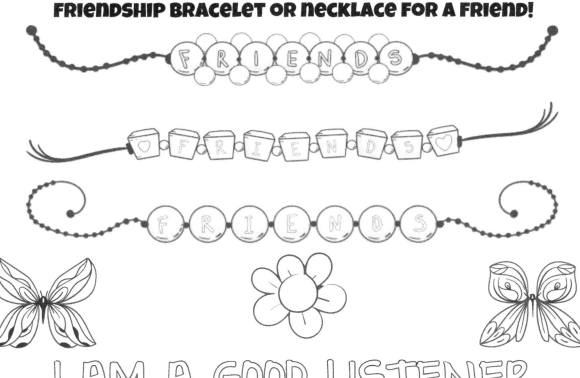

I AM A GOOD LISTENER

I FEEL: 😄 🙂 🙂 😐 🙁 ☹️ 😣

COLOR YOUR MOOD TODAY

DATE: ___/___/___   M   T   W   TH   F   SAT   SUN

BEING KIND TO OTHERS IS FREE

SOMETHING I WILL IMPROVE ON TODAY... _____

DRAW SOMETHING THAT MAKES YOU PROUD

TWO THINGS I AM THANKFUL FOR TODAY

① _____

② _____

I FEEL: 😃   🙂   🙂   😐   🙁   🙁   ☹️

COLOR YOUR MOOD TODAY

DATE: ___/___/___   M   T   W   TH   F   SAT   SUN

I FORGIVE MYSELF FOR THE MISTAKES I MAKE

TWO THINGS I AM THANKFUL FOR TODAY

① _____

② _____

DRAW YOUR FAVORITE ANIMAL

TODAY I AM PROUD THAT... _____

_____

"NO MATTER HOW SMALL, NO ACT OF KINDNESS IS WASTED"

I FEEL: 😀 🙂 🙂 😐 🙁 🙁 🙁

COLOR YOUR MOOD TODAY

DATE: ___/___/___   M   T   W   TH   F   SAT   SUN

I WILL SAY WHEN
I WANT TO

THE BRAVEST PERSON I KNOW IS... _____

I ADMIRE THEM BECAUSE... _____

DRAW THE PEOPLE, PLACES, OR THINGS YOU ARE GRATEFUL FOR THAT
STARTS WITH THE LETTER "P"

I FEEL: 😀 🙂 🙂 😐 🙁 ☹️ 😦

COLOR YOUR MOOD TODAY

I AM SO UNSELFISH

WHEN I NEED ADVICE A PERSON I CAN ALWAYS RELY ON IS... _____

_____

DRAW THE WEATHER TODAY AND WRITE SOMETHING YOU APPRECIATED ABOUT IT

TWO THINGS I AM THANKFUL FOR TODAY

1 _____

2 _____

I FEEL: 😀 🙂 🙂 😐 🙁 🙁 😧

COLOR YOUR MOOD TODAY

DATE: ___/___/___   M   T   W   TH   F   SAT   SUN

I FEEL: COLOR YOUR MOOD TODAY

"I OFFER A UNIQUE PERSPECTIVE"

I'M THANKFUL FOR TODAY BECAUSE... _____

_____

Reflection of Gratitude

ACT OF GRATITUDE

YOU ARE PERFECT THE WAY YOU ARE!

STAND IN FRONT OF A MIRROR AND APPRECIATE EVERYTHING ABOUT YOURSELF.
MAKE A LIST OF THE THINGS YOU SEE THAT YOU LOVE.
PRACTICE THIS EACH MORNING FOR 5 DAYS.

ALL MY PROBLEMS HAVE SOLUTIONS

I FEEL: 😄 🙂 🙂 😐 🙁 🙁 ☹️

COLOR YOUR MOOD TODAY

DATE: ___/___/___ M T W TH F SAT SUN

I AM NOT ALONE

DRAW SOMEONE YOU ADMIRE AND ARE GRATEFUL FOR

THREE THINGS I ADMIRE ABOUT MY PARENTS ARE... _____

_____

_____

"DIFFICULT IS HARD BUT NOT IMPOSSIBLE"

I FEEL: 😄 🙂 🙂 😐 😕 🙁 ☹️

COLOR YOUR MOOD TODAY

DATE: ___/___/___   M   T   W   TH   F   SAT   SUN

I AM WELL-RESTED
AND FULL OF ENERGY

THE LAST JOKE THAT MADE ME LAUGH WAS... _____

_____

DRAW THE PEOPLE, PLACES, OR THINGS YOU ARE GRATEFUL FOR THAT
STARTS WITH THE LETTER "I"

I

I FEEL: 😀 🙂 🙂 😐 🙁 ☹️ 😧

COLOR YOUR MOOD TODAY

DATE: ___/___/___   M   T   W   TH   F   SAT   SUN

OPPORTUNITIES ARE EVERYWHERE

A CHALLENGE I'M DEALING WITH RIGHT NOW IS

_____

FROM THIS SITUATION I'M LEARNING _____

_____

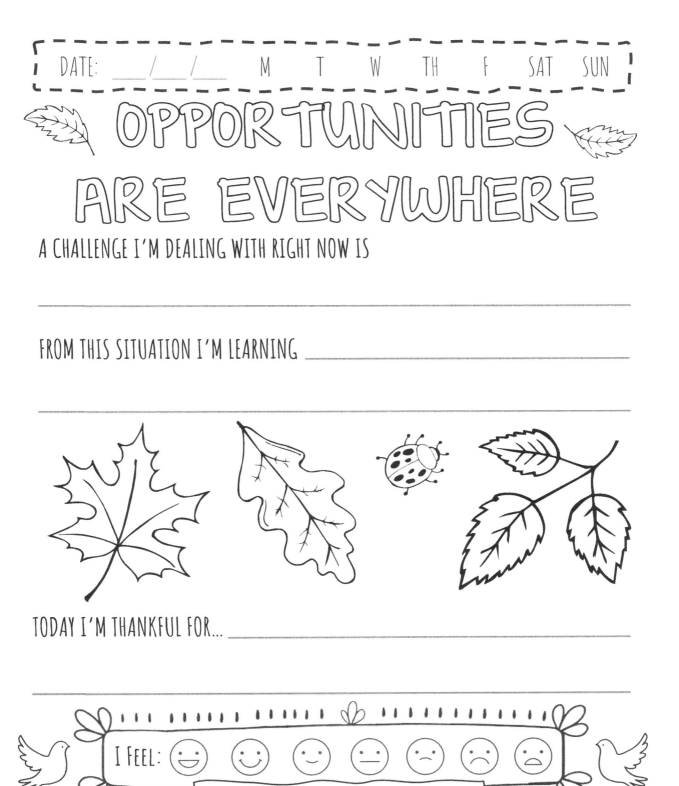

TODAY I'M THANKFUL FOR... _____

I FEEL: 😄 🙂 🙂 😐 🙁 ☹️ 😦

COLOR YOUR MOOD TODAY

DATE: ___/___/___ M T W TH F SAT SUN

I'M THANKFUL FOR TODAY BECAUSE... _____

"I HAVE A BRAVE HEART"

I FEEL: 😄 🙂 🙂 😐 🙁 ☹️ 😣

COLOR YOUR MOOD TODAY

♡ I ACCEPT MYSELF ♡

DRAW OR WRITE ABOUT A PERFECT DAY YOU HAD

THE LAST TIME SOMEONE FORGAVE ME WAS... _____

_____

AND IT MADE ME FEEL... _____

_____

"ANYTHING IS POSSIBLE"

I FEEL: 😄 🙂 🙂 😐 🙁 ☹️ 😧

COLOR YOUR MOOD TODAY

DATE: ___ / ___ / ___   M   T   W   TH   F   SAT   SUN

I AM COMPASSION

THE BEST THING ABOUT MY DAY WAS... _____

_____

DRAW THE PEOPLE, PLACES, OR THINGS YOU ARE GRATEFUL FOR THAT STARTS WITH THE LETTER "D"

I FEEL: 😄 🙂 🙂 😐 🙁 🙁 🙁

COLOR YOUR MOOD TODAY

Free Audio

7-Minute Guided Meditation for Girls

Gratitude | Happiness | Confidence | Self Love

including 8 powerful affirmations!

Meditation is known to:

• Improve focus and attention
• Reduce stress and anxiety
• Improve emotional regulation
• Improve sleep
• Increase overall well-being and happiness.

http://bit.ly/3HvlL6W

Made in the USA
Monee, IL
15 June 2023

35887196R00059